How
To
Scam

And make lots of money.

This book is a necessary read both for persons who see a living through scamming and for persons who want to avoid scammers. Failure to read this book is failure to get rich quick or avoid scammers.

This is a book for educational purpose. Get rich by reading it now or don't read it and get scammed. The choice is yours.

Preface

Before you get some effective ways to scam, here are several rules about being a scammer that you must first know:

Look genuine

(Rule 1)

Your appearance is the first thing that advertises you to others. When you walk on the street and see each individual, you have an assumption of who they are because of how they dress. How many times have you walked on the street and assume that someone is a teacher, thug, Christian, prostitute, etc. because of the way that person dressed?

So if you are scamming in person, you must look the part of whatever you are pretending to be.

Appearance is not just about clothes. It applies to any thing that the person you are about to scam will see---including the following:

a. <u>Hair</u> (your hair cut or hairstyle must fit in with your deception. Are you posing as a sales man? Then your hair cannot look like a garbage collector.

b. <u>Shoes</u> (wear a pair of shoes that fits in with what you are pretending to be. Are you posing as a child care agent from the government to swindle money from someone who would not want the government to take away her child? Then the shoes you wear could not be sneakers.

c. <u>Website</u> (your website must look convincing. Nowadays, many individuals read about a company by first going to their website).

d. Email (Your email address must look convincing. It does not matter if you create it at Yahoo, Gmail, Hotmail or another host. The point is that your email address must be worded to fit in with your deception. Are you running a fake investment business? Then an email address such as Hotboy45@Yahoo.com will not work. The email address must appear business-like such as, for example: investor@MoneyMarketOffshore.com

Sound Genuine

(Rule 2)

People judge you by the way you sound. People judge your weakness, strength, confidence, maturity, education, social affiliation, friendliness, meanness, mental health, and nationality by the sound of your voice.

To ensure you sound genuine, you will need to apply the following:

a. Sound confident: A scammer must at all times sound confident in what he is saying. This means that you must not let the person you are targeting think that you are not sure about what you are saying or that you are worried he or she will not believe you. Don't let the person smell a sense of fear in you or get the impression that you are inexperience. You must sound strong.

   If you want to maintain a friendly voice over the phone, keep smiling while you speak.

b. Sound mature: You will most likely not succeed if you sound immature (childish). To sound mature, you must avoid grinning._ You can smile, but under no circumstance should you be grinning. Also, you must not laugh unnecessarily.

c. <u>Use the right tone:</u>   How your voice sounds will affect the thinking of the person you are talking with. So you must use the right tone of voice in a particular situation. You do not want to sound threatening when you should sound friendly. You do not want to sound childish when you should sound business-like.

d. <u>Choose your words carefully:</u> If you are running a fake business, your use of words (in writing and verbally) must fit the type of business that you are faking.

   Remember, words are powerful. You must choose them well so that you do not sound desperate or offend the person you are dealing with.

Be Patient

(Rule 3)

You must be patient. Yes, you want 'quick money.' But if you push too hard, the individual you are targeting may get suspicious.

Being patient does not mean that you must take things slow. The longer you take to secure the money, the more likely it may be for the person to have a change of mind.

If the person says "I am having second thoughts about this," you can say "I want you to take your time. There is no need to rush. Why are you doubtful?"

The method is to get the money fast without appearing fast. What does this mean? This means that you will develop a procedure through which you will get the money fast and not make the individual feel pushed to act.

How to develop your procedure

You will develop your procedure by making the individual the priority of the whole process. You will let the individual believe that by acting quickly their action will benefit mainly them. You will let the individual believe that it is up to them to act to better themselves.

Here are some things you should not do during your procedure of scamming:

1. Do not immediately go into asking for money. You must first develop the state of trust between you and the individual, and this means that you will have to:

    (a) Make the person feel relaxed talking with you,

    (b) Highlight the benefit the person would receive after sending you the money.

    Not every call you make to the individual must be about getting them to send you the money. By getting the individual to like, trust and believe in you, the money will come.

2. Do not quickly get aggressive and threatening if you feel that things are not going to work in your favour.

If you will use threat, it may not work with anyone. Threats typically work best (or easier) when you are scamming a weak-minded person or a rich and old person.

There are few ways to go about using threat to get the individual you are targeting to act:

(a) Tell him or her where they live and that he or she wouldn't want you to do what you have done to a lady before. Tell the individual: "I wouldn't want you, or someone close to you, to go missing the same way too."

Never tell the person exactly what you will do. Why? If you tell the person that you will kidnap them, for example, he or she will measure the possibility of that. If he or she knows that they are in a position where they can't be kidnapped, they won't feel threatened by you. Keeping the person uncertain about what you would do makes your threat effective.

(b) Your threat will work if you have gathered some information about the individual. If you can't tell the person their name, or where he or she lives, or where he or she works, that person will not feel that you have the ability to harm them.

(c) **Threaten with care**. What does this mean? When you are threatening the individual, let the person feel that it is up to him or her to do what you want (send the money) in order to not get hurt. For example, you may say: "I don't want to take you out. But it is up to you to not get eliminated like the others."

(d) **Never threaten with an angry voice.** You don't want to be considered as blustering. Instead, you must sound rather calm and serious---which will make you sound like a dangerous and heartless person.

(e) **Never actually carry out your threat.** You are a scammer, not a murderer. You can do things to galvanize the individual to act—such as leave a threatening note on their car window, give a threatening message to their child (or grandchild) to give them, go to their work place and observe what they are doing and call and tell them later.

The point is that if the person feels that you have access to him or her (or a beloved family member), the person will act in your favour out of fear.

The following pages in this book will show you some effective ways to scam and not stay broke.

PayPal

There is more than one way to use PayPal to scam PayPal itself. Here are two effective ways:

The first option

1. Create two PayPal accounts. One will be in a fake name and the other in your own name or the name of someone you know.

2. Verify each account with an Entropay virtual Visa card (visit Entropay.com to sign up for free and buy the cards).

3. Offer something for sale using the fake PayPal account. [Don't use eBay.com as the money won't get to you fast enough]. When a purchase is made, sign into the fake account and transfer the money to the other PayPal account.

(You must not use the same computer to sign into both accounts—because this will draw the suspicion of PayPal).

Abandon the fake account after this as PayPal will put it under its radar (watch) and it will have a negative balance.

The second option

1. Create two PayPal accounts. One in your name and the other in the name of a friend.

2. Verify each account with an Entropay virtual Visa card (visit Entropay.com to sign up for free and buy the cards).

3. Load a thousand dollars (or more/less) in the PayPal account in your name.

4. Create a Google site or blog and offer a product for sale at $1000 – using your friend's PayPal account.

5. Buy the product off the Google site or blog using the $1000 you have in your own PayPal account.

6. Withdraw the money from your friend's account. Then make a complaint to PayPal (within the time PayPal offer buyers to do so) that you have not received the item you bought. PayPal will eventually refund the $1000 to your account. You will now have your original $1000 back—plus the amount you have withdrawn from your friend's PayPal account!

   You must abandon the account in your friend's name after this. Because this account now falls under the radar of PayPal, you must not sign into it on your own computer.

Fake Tickets

You can make money by selling fake concert tickets online. You will do this by advertising tickets for an upcoming concert. It is better to target the shows (live performances) of very popular celebrities. For example: Beyounce and Justin Beiber.

How to sell

1. Find out when and where the next popular stage shows will be held. You can find out through their advertisements and also through research on Google. Get all the information about the show — location, date; ticket costs.

2. Place an advertisement online (example: on Facebook) for persons to buy tickets to the show.

3. You can create a website to sell the ticket or simply create a form at **Jotform.com** to sell. Jotform is free and you can use the link on the form in your advertisement.

4. Sell the tickets for less (about 10% less) than the cost of the real tickets. If you are targeting a Justin Beiber's stage show, for example, advertise the tickets in more than one country (Canada, USA, UK).

Fake Fundraiser

Many individuals raise money online for different causes. Many individuals donate to such causes.

You can scam donors by posting a fake cause online. There are several online fundraising websites that you can use to do this---such Fundly.com, Hero network, and Youcaring.com.

<u>The best way</u>

You can post a real fundraiser on any of the above-named website and nobody gives you a dime. As a scammer, it is not your place to be real. You will go fake with your fundraising. You will create a fake fundraiser by doing the following:

a. Get the latest news in America, Canada or the UK. Find a recent tragedy that makes the news (best if it makes the news on BBC, CBS, CNN, or another famous news channel).

b. Let's say you see a piece of news about a little girl who met in a car accident and is in hospital. The news is fresh and many persons are sympathizing with the family. Don't linger. You will right away create a post on one of the fundraising websites (example: Youcaring.com) and start raising funds. Use a picture of the accident and/or victim in the fundraiser.

c. Do not use one fundraising website. Use as many as you can in order to reach more donors.

d. Advertise the fundraiser online (Facebook, Craiglist, Twitter, Tumblr, Google+, etc).

Facebook Fake Profile

Facebook is a place to make new friends, and it is also a great place to easily scam money. With Facebook, you can create multiple profiles for various purposes---one or more for scamming.

How to scam on Facebook

(Option one)

    a. Visit a website that lists the names and photos of US soldiers. Choose a picture of a young soldier (get more pictures of him if you can—on Facebook, Google search, Twitter, etc).

    b. Create a Facebook profile with the photo (or photos) of the soldier. Do not use his real name as you do not want to conflict with his real Facebook profile. Make sure the age you use match the photo.

c. Send friend requests to American females you know or assume have lots of money. Typically, Americans have lots of respect for guys in the US Army and won't deny a friend request. Communicate with your American female friends regularly for at least two months.

(Do not sign in and chat too often each week, because you don't want to appear idle. Also, make sure that you use words that make you appear like a real soldier. For example: When you are referring to the military, use pronouns such as 'us,' 'we,' and 'me and the guys' instead of pronouns like 'them,' 'they').

d. Zero in on some of your rich American friends and develop a closer friendship.

(Don't tell them that you are presently posted overseas or that you are an imputed veteran back home. Instead, you are back from Afghanistan for four months. A guy who is still active in the army is more appealing).

e. To scam money, tell each friend—in private chat-- that your mother (your mom) is sick with her heart. Do not ask for money yet. Each friend will sympathize. Chat with each friend about how your mom was your main supporter in joining the army and serving your country and that seeing her sick makes you sad.

When each friend begins to ask about the present condition of your mom, tell them that she needs to do a surgery and you are thinking about raising money to assist with her care. If a friend does not voluntarily offer to help financially, you should ask the friend if she would like to assist. If asked how much you want to raise in amount, tell the friend US$2000 but she can give any amount to help.

f. If you live outside the United States, you cannot ask the friends to send money by check or Western Union to you. If you ask them to send money outside the United States, they will get suspicious and refuse. Therefore you will have to use an international money processer—such as PayPal or Skrill to receive the money. Scam as many persons on your friend list as possible. Keep chatting with them a little after they send you money until you are ready to delete the account.

How To Scam on Facebook

(Option two)

- A. Find and use the photos of a very good-looking female off Twitter, Tagged, or another social website. (Don't use the photos of a professional model as this will expose your fake).

- B. Create a fake Facebook profile with such photos. Do not use the real name of the person whose photos you are using. Give a name, age, profession or school, and personality to the fake profile.

- C. Befriend men on Facebook from other countries who look like they have lots of money. (Look for signs of riches in the men by look at their profession, clothes, and background in their photos).

D. Zero in on some of the men by being friendly (but not appear slutty) to develop a close relationship.

E. Ask for money when you have changed the friendship between you and each man into an online relationship. (Make sure that none of the men on your friend list is a friend to another on the list. Also, add females to you friend list so that you don't appear like a slut).

Fake accommodation

People love to travel. And when many persons travel, they pay for accommodation where they go. Millions of dollars are earned each year from providing accommodation at a cost. Hoteliers become rich along with small guesthouse owners in the same business. Wouldn't you want to earn from the flow of money in providing accommodation?

Since your answer is yes, do the following:

(Option one)

1. Find a country from a region in the world that gets a lot of tourist visitors.

2. Create a website (at Google site, Webs, or Weebly, etc) and put it under a domain. Get some pictures of a nice building — whether off the internet or snap some photos yourself. Post the pictures on the website along with information about the place---such as amenities (air-condition bedroom, etc.), location, costs per night, owner's name, and so on.

3. When the website is finished and looks convincing, you will start advertise your accommodation service (on Facebook, Google Adwords, etc.) to persons in other countries.

4. Ensure that you let persons pay at the time they book for accommodation on the website. Use more than one payment option—such as PayPal, Western Union, Payoneer.

(Option Two)

The football world cup, world cup cricket, and the Olympics draw a lot of persons to the location where to be held. These games cause hotels to be fully booked and some fans have to sleep in cars, etc. The best time to advertise a fake accommodation is during a world cup or the Olympics. The procedure is pretty much the same as option one above:

1. At least a month before the event, create a website or a form at Jotform.com. Post photos and information about your fake place. (the location you put must be close to the event)

2. Set a cost per night for staying at your place.

3. If you live in the same country where the world cup or the Olympics will be held, you can accept payment via MoneyGram and Western Union. If you live outside the country, your best choice of accepting payment will be PayPal or Skrill.

4. Advertise your accommodation online and even in overseas papers. You can also create a Facebook page for your fake accommodation.

5. The earlier you start to advertise the better. For the world cup or the Olympics, you can easily get over 200 persons paying to stay at your place. If you are renting a room for US$80 per night, and you get 325 persons who pay, the total amount you get would be US$26000.

Craiglist Post

(Illegal items)

A scammer is a part of the underworld. Persons in the illegal gun and drug trade have to carry out their activities secretly. Such inability of criminals to get away from the 'secret dealings' of the underworld, works in favour of a scammer.

Many criminals (or criminal-minded persons) want to own a gun. You can make some money from the fake sale of a gun, as follows:

i. Get a new sim card for this purpose only.
ii. Post a 'Gun For Sale' advertisement on Craiglist, (and other similar sites too) along with a picture of a particular handgun with information about it and email address.
iii. When you are contacted, tell the person you only accept cash. Tell them that for you to enure he's not a cop, you will accept payment through Western Union and then you will leave the weapon at a location of their choice or send it by mail.

Give the person the phone number to call you if he's serious.

Over the phone, you must not sound weak. State your position—that the person has to pay first through Western Union and then get the weapon via mail or you will leave it at a spot chosen by him.

It doesn't matter that you will give the person your real name. You don't have to be specific about your address with Western Union. For example, your information given to the person to use at Western Union can look like the following:

Mark Blair
Bradford, Connecticut.

The person can't find your specific address with this unspecific information.

Fake Psychic

Everyone wants to be safe. The fear of the unknown can be a very strong fear. As a scammer, you can act on this fear in your favour by pretending to be a psychic. The best way to do this is as follows:

1. Find the phone number of someone who is rich. This can be done from the telephone directory. (There are some areas where only rich and wealthy persons live). You will target those areas.

2. Call the person and tell him (or her) that his life is in danger. When the person asks you what you mean, explain that you see him or her meeting in a car accident (or about to be killed by a close person to him). Before the person can say anything, you must quickly tell him or her that you have seen this kind of thing happened with a man before from (give a distant location) and the man never heeded your warning and ended up dead.

3. Tell the person that you can see dangers and that you can help him save himself from the impending death.

4. Because you know the person's address from the phone directory, tell the person that you would come to his (just name of town or community) but you will stay where you are and read the dangers and tell him. Warn the person to be careful in the next two weeks.

5. Don't answer any questions the person asks about who you are. Tell him or her that you want to save him from the tragic death ahead but in this world everything takes money even if you don't want it.

6. Ask the person if he or she believes in God. No matter what the person's answer is, go right into telling the person you want to save his life but you charge a small amount to continue carry out your vital service. State the amount the person should pay you. (US$ 100 is not too low or high).

7. Call more than one rich person. But do not do this too many times in the same town as persons communicate with each other.

8. Collect money via bank deposit, Western Union, or—if the person wishes to pay in person—cash.

Thanks for reading

Now go and make some money.

www.ingramcontent.com/pod-product-compliance
Lightning Source LLC
Chambersburg PA
CBHW070522290526
45790CB00003B/1270